AMERICA AT WAR

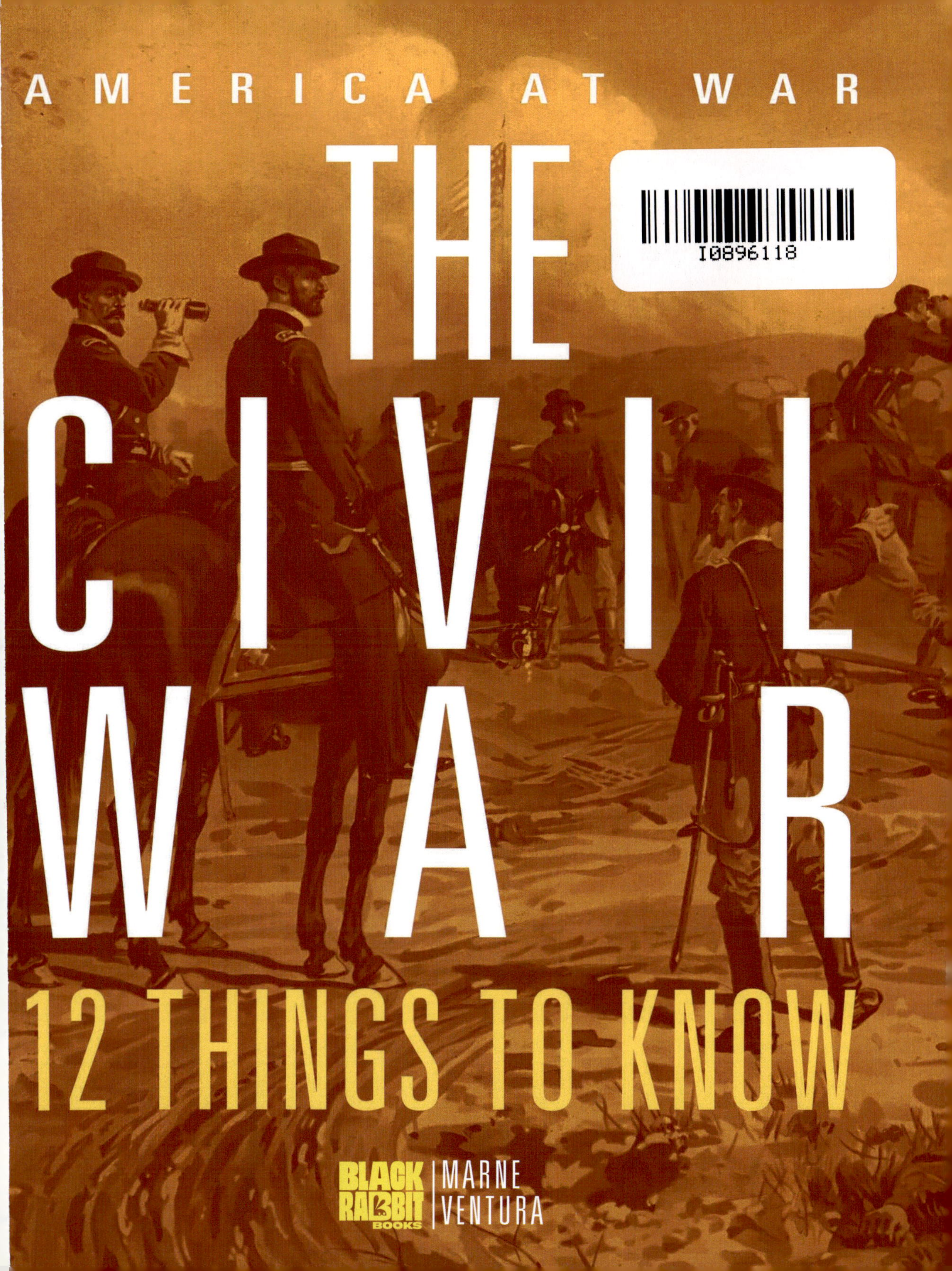

THE CIVIL WAR

12 THINGS TO KNOW

BLACK RABBIT BOOKS

MARNE VENTURA

Table of Contents

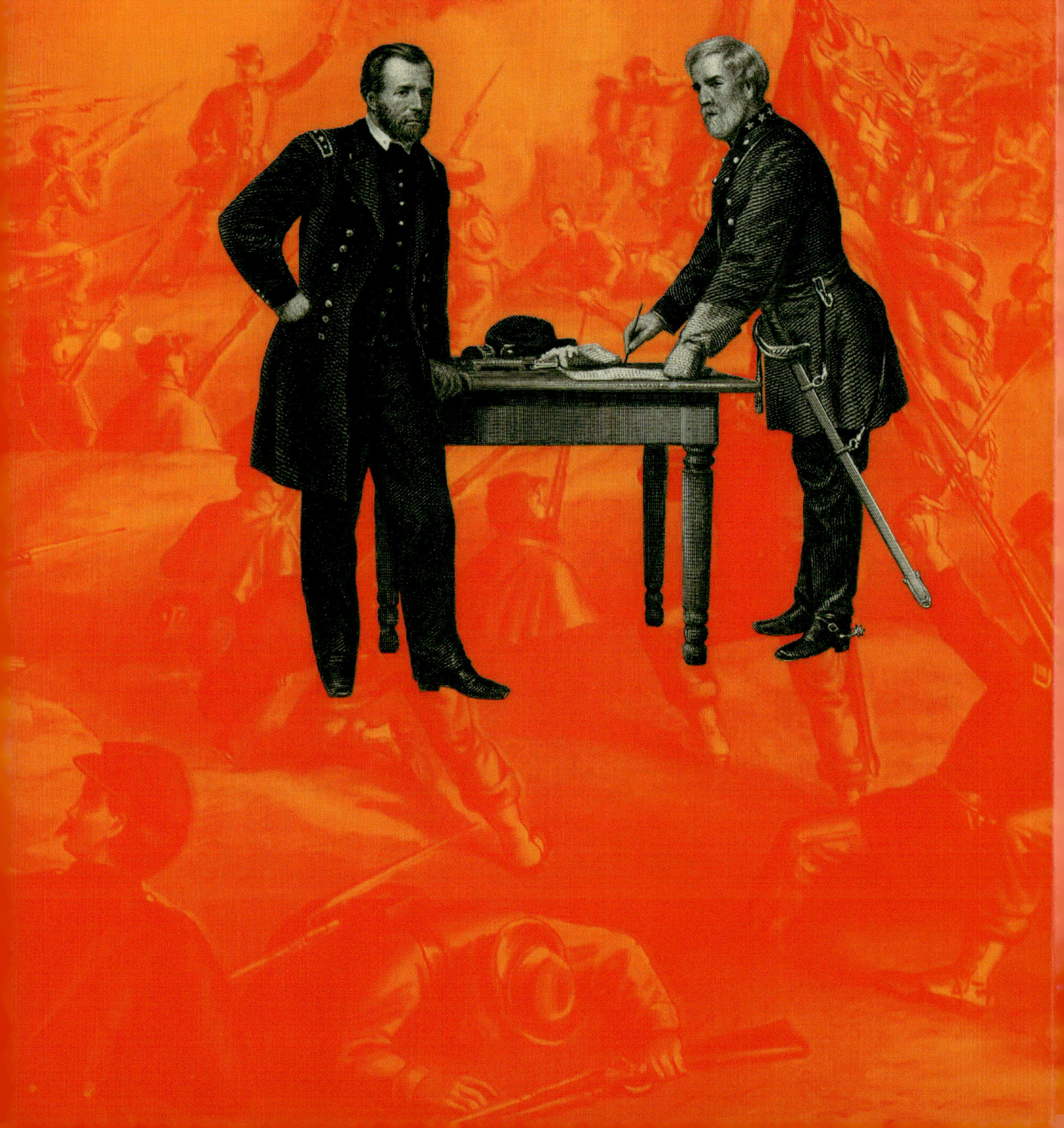

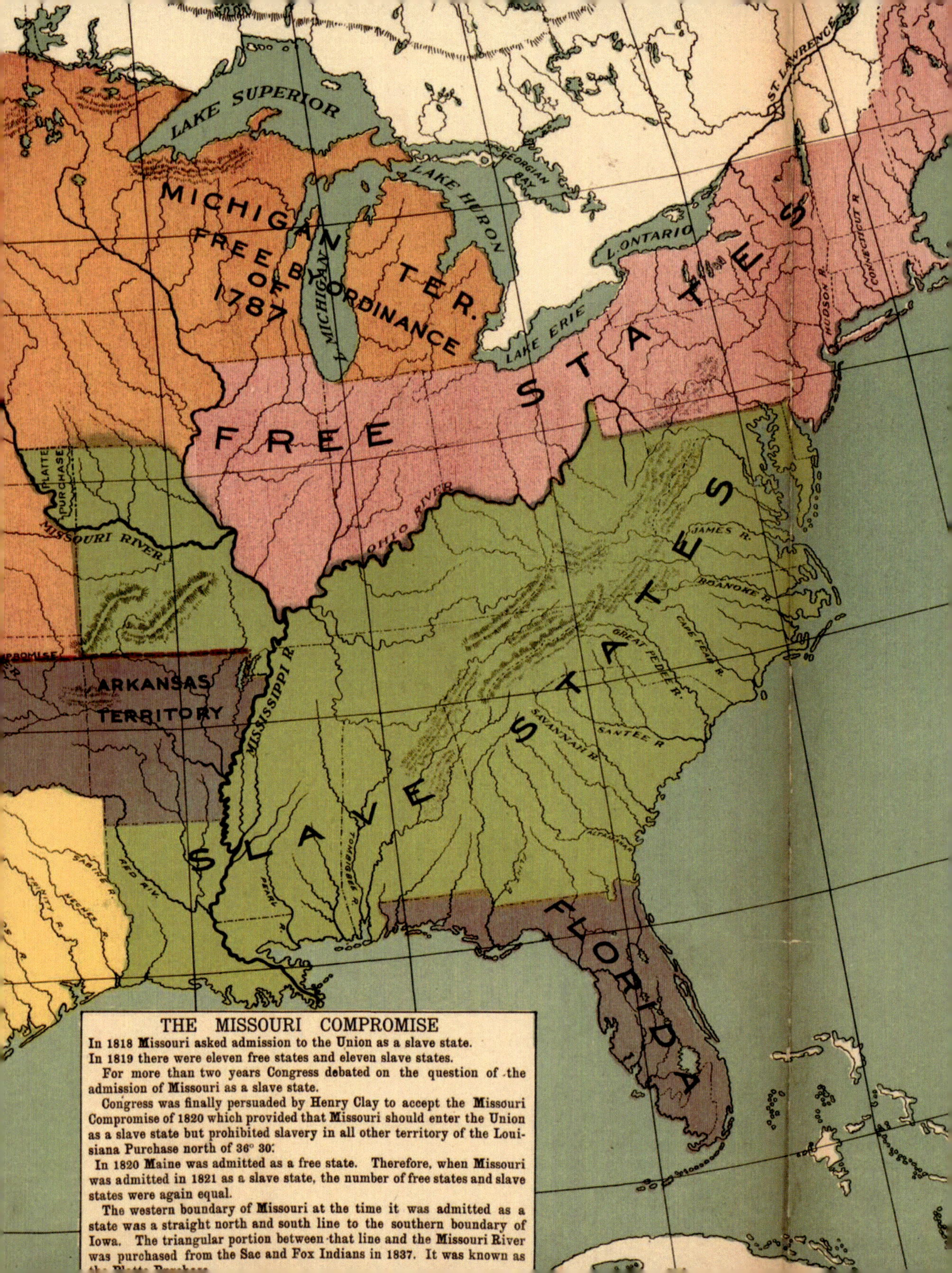

THE MISSOURI COMPROMISE

In 1818 Missouri asked admission to the Union as a slave state.

In 1819 there were eleven free states and eleven slave states.

For more than two years Congress debated on the question of the admission of Missouri as a slave state.

Congress was finally persuaded by Henry Clay to accept the Missouri Compromise of 1820 which provided that Missouri should enter the Union as a slave state but prohibited slavery in all other territory of the Louisiana Purchase north of 36° 30'.

In 1820 Maine was admitted as a free state. Therefore, when Missouri was admitted in 1821 as a slave state, the number of free states and slave states were again equal.

The western boundary of Missouri at the time it was admitted as a state was a straight north and south line to the southern boundary of Iowa. The triangular portion between that line and the Missouri River was purchased from the Sac and Fox Indians in 1837. It was known as

North and South Disagree *over Slavery*

1

America in the 1800s was much different than it is today. In 1804, there were only 17 states. That number grew to 33 by 1859. In the North, people mostly lived in cities. In the South, most people were farmers. Enslaved people were forced to work on **plantations**. The North did not rely on slave labor. But the South did. Some slaves escaped to the North to live. This caused tension between the states.

The country was growing. It was expanding west. As new states formed, they argued over slavery laws. Congress tried to keep the peace. It passed a **compromise** in 1820. It is known as the Missouri Compromise. This drew an imaginary line across the old Louisiana Territory. People north of the line could not hold slaves.

But the South still could. For the time, there was an equal number of slave and anti-slave states.

New laws mostly kept the balance. But in 1854, the scale tipped. A new act opened land north of the imaginary line to allow slaves. People in the West could now vote on slavery. The act also **repealed** the Missouri Compromise. In 1857, the Supreme Court upheld this decision. It ruled that the compromise was **unconstitutional**. It said Black people were not US **citizens**. The ruling opened all territories to slavery. The North was outraged. Tensions grew. Soon, a war was brewing.

4 million Number of enslaved people living in the South in 1860.

The American Anti-Slavery Society was formed in Boston. • The group made a newspaper. • They wrote about how badly enslaved people were treated. • People against slavery were called abolitionists.

Anti-Slavery Society Convention, June 1840

7

Southern States Leave *the Union*

2

Abraham Lincoln

Abraham Lincoln ran for president in 1860. He was part of the Republican Party. It did not support slavery. The Democratic Party was split over the issue. Small groups started breaking off. They formed new parties. It seemed like no one could agree. Lincoln said, “A house divided against itself cannot stand.” Americans needed to find a way to agree about slavery.

The US government was called the Union. The South was afraid the Union would ban all slavery. That would ruin the Southern economy. They needed workers to keep their plantations running. The South believed slave labor was a state’s right. The North was a threat to their way of life. The only way to keep their right was to separate from the Union.

On December 20, 1860, South Carolina **seceded**. By February 1861, six other states did the same. Leaders

THINK ABOUT IT

What factors led to the start of the American Civil War?

A group of enslaved men and women prepare sweet potatoes for planting.

of these states met in Alabama. They formed a new government. It was called the Confederate States of America. Jefferson Davis was elected president. He was a senator from Mississippi. Lincoln won the presidency of the Union. He would take office in 1861.

The Confederacy said the 10th **Amendment** gave them the right to leave. Lincoln did not agree. He saw it as an act of **treason**. He thought it would destroy the Union. The North felt betrayed. They did not accept the Confederacy as a new country.

Union flag

Confederate flag

11 Total number of states that seceded from the Union.

The South left to protect their state rights. • The Confederate capital was in Richmond, Virginia. The Confederate capital was in Richmond, Virginia.
- Some Northerners were fine with the South leaving.
- Some Southerners wanted to stay with the Union.

The Civil War Begins at *Fort Sumter*

3

Confederate soldiers began taking over forts in the South. James Buchanan was at the end of his presidential term. He would not give up the forts without a fight.

Union Major Robert Anderson was stationed at Fort Moultrie in Charleston, South Carolina. He had less than 90 men. They could not defend against a land attack. On December 26, 1860, Anderson took action. He moved his men to Fort Sumter. It was a much bigger fort.

Anderson and his men were low on supplies. Several missions to bring them more had failed. This was President Lincoln's first major crisis. He had to figure out how to resupply Fort Sumter. He tried to send a ship with food. The Confederates fired on it. They would not let it go through. They told Anderson to leave the fort.

Anderson stayed put. On April 12, 1861, the Confederates fired on the fort. They attacked for 34 hours. Anderson's men tried to fight back. There was little they could do. On April 13, Union forces surrendered.

Lincoln accused the Confederate states of **insurrection**. This gave him the right to use force against them. On April 15, he called for 75,000 volunteers to join the Union Army. He ordered a **blockade** of Southern ports. This made it hard to trade cotton. The South could not make weapons. And now they couldn't get war supplies from other countries.

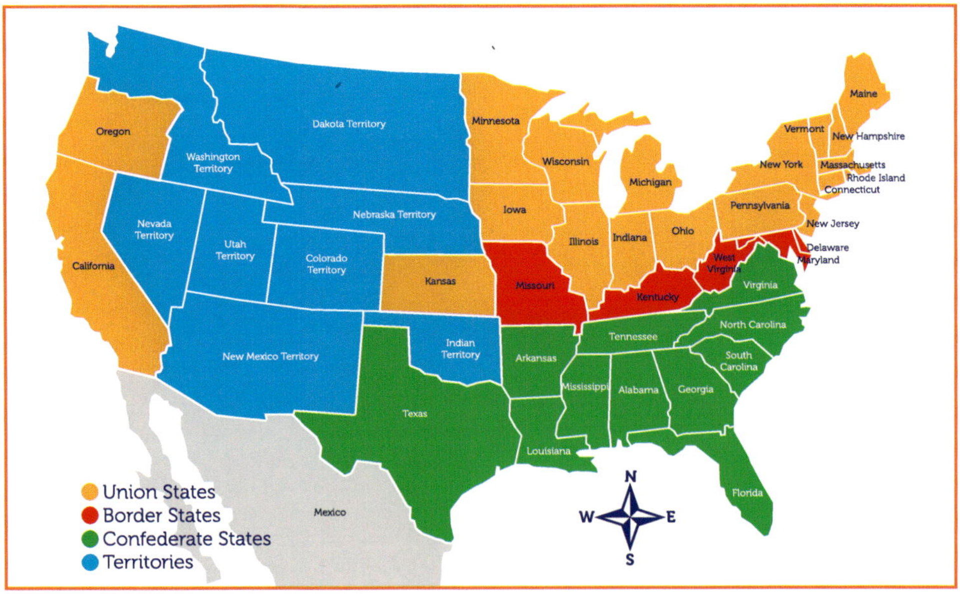

85 Number of Union soldiers stationed in South Carolina when it seceded.

The Confederate General at Fort Sumter was P. G. T. Beauregard. • The Union soldiers were poorly armed. • Fort Sumter was the first battle in the Civil War. No one lost their life.

The Gatling gun—an early machine gun—was first used in the Civil War.

Union Fails to End the *War Quickly*

4

Lincoln's blockade was in effect. The Union controlled the ports and waterways. The South could not trade with Europe. With few factories, it could not make weapons or supplies. Lincoln thought this would make the South give up.

Union General Winfield Scott built off this idea. He came up with the Anaconda Plan. The plan had two main goals. The first was to continue the blockade. The second was to send troops down the Mississippi River. They would capture forts along the way. The Confederacy would be split into two groups. It would then soon surrender.

General Scott's plan came from the idea that snakes slowly squeeze their prey to death.

Scott's plan would take time. He thought it might take two years or more. Union leaders thought that was too long. They wanted it over in a few months. One big battle, they said, would decide it all. Many parts of Scott's plan were set aside. Others were put into action later.

16,000 Number of Union troops at the start of the war.

Scott thought the Union would need at least 300,000 troops. • Bull Run was the first full-scale battle of the Civil War. • Union leaders wanted the war over in 90 days. That did not happen.

Battle of Bull Run was the first major battle of the war.

THINK ABOUT IT

What are three possible reasons the Union leaders wanted the war to end in 90 days?

By June 1861, four more Southern states had left the Union. They made Richmond, Virginia, the Confederate capital. President Lincoln pushed his generals to capture this city. He saw a chance for a quick end to the war.

Union troops marched to Richmond. Confederate troops met them in Bull Run. They fought on July 21, 1861. As planned, there was a big battle. But it did not end the war. The Union retreated to Washington, DC. They realized the war would last longer than they thought.

Union Army Captures *Fort Henry*

5

Civil War storage barrels held food supplies.

In the fall of 1861, Union leaders made another move. They wanted control of the rivers west of the Appalachian Mountains. Winning them would cut off supply lines to the South. They were also after Fort Henry in Tennessee. This would open a water route to the South. Union troops could easily reach the center of the country.

On February 6, 1862, the Union Army attacked Fort Henry. They were led by led by Ulysses S. Grant and Andrew Foote. They had 15,000 troops. They also had gunboats. There were only 2,800 Confederates. They only had rifles and old guns.

The Union gunboats moved in close to the fort. They damaged Confederate defenses. The Confederates fought back. They were able to take out one of the gunboats. The Union lost 32 soldiers. The Confederates lost 21 soldiers. They also lost most of their guns.

The Southerners said they would surrender. However, they didn't actually give up. Their leader was General Lloyd Tilghman. He had secretly moved some of his troops to Fort Donelson. It was 12 miles (19 kilometers) away. Ten days later, the Union captured that fort as well.

These battles were key wins for the Union. They now controlled the Cumberland and Tennessee Rivers. They moved troops and supplies along the rivers. The Confederates were not able to use them for the rest of the war.

Union Navy gunboat

The Battle of Fort Donelson helped the Union take control of Kentucky and most of Tennessee.

82 Number of Confederate soldiers who surrendered at Fort Henry.

The Union had four ironclad ships and three wooden ships. • The Confederates' guns were from the War of 1812. • Many of the Confederate troops were ill.

The storage and capture of food supplies can greatly impact an army's success.

Battle of Antietam Is the Bloodiest Day *of the War*

6

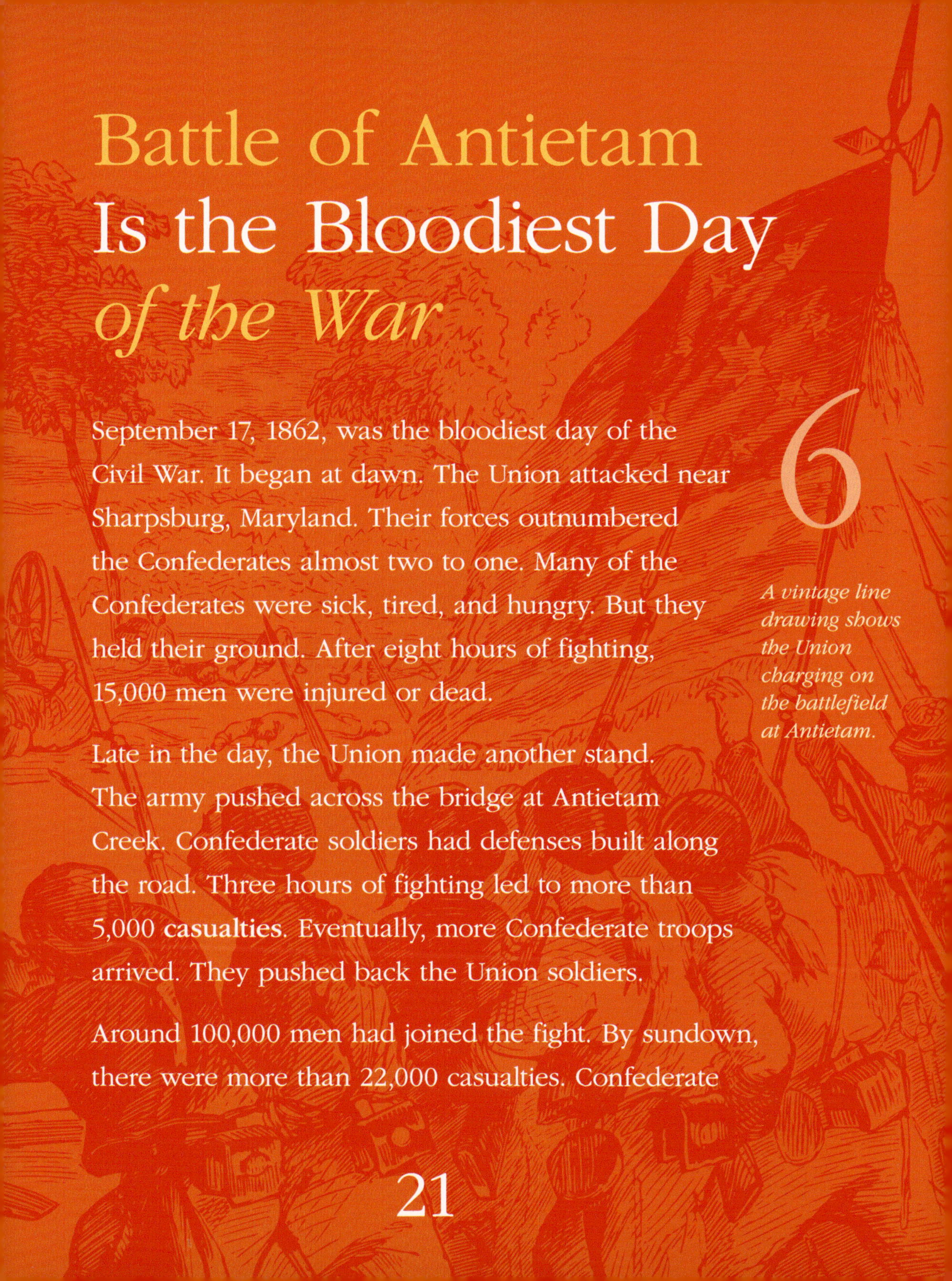

A vintage line drawing shows the Union charging on the battlefield at Antietam.

September 17, 1862, was the bloodiest day of the Civil War. It began at dawn. The Union attacked near Sharpsburg, Maryland. Their forces outnumbered the Confederates almost two to one. Many of the Confederates were sick, tired, and hungry. But they held their ground. After eight hours of fighting, 15,000 men were injured or dead.

Late in the day, the Union made another stand. The army pushed across the bridge at Antietam Creek. Confederate soldiers had defenses built along the road. Three hours of fighting led to more than 5,000 **casualties**. Eventually, more Confederate troops arrived. They pushed back the Union soldiers.

Around 100,000 men had joined the fight. By sundown, there were more than 22,000 casualties. Confederate

General Robert E. Lee did not surrender. He just marched back to Virginia. The Battle of Antietam ended in a draw.

President Lincoln claimed the battle as a win for the Union. He felt it put him in a strong position to take a stand against slavery. He promised to free the slaves in all states on January 1, 1863.

CLARA BARTON

At the start of the war, Clara Barton worked in a government office. She wanted to help soldiers. She risked her life to take supplies to the field. She cared for the sick and wounded. Barton became a folk hero for her service as a nurse. She earned the nickname "Angel of the Battlefield."

Civil War reenactors act out the events of the Antietam battle.

4,000 Number of men who died in the Battle of Antietam.

President Lincoln shared the Emancipation Proclamation on September 22, 1862. • It said the South must stop fighting. • When the South did not stop, Lincoln said all slaves are free.

Lee's Confederates Win Battle *of Fredericksburg*

7

It was the end of 1862. The North and South were still at war. Union General Ambrose Burnside had 120,000 men. He ordered them to cross the Rappahannock River. They were on their way to Richmond, Virginia. The river was too deep to cross on foot. The men had to wait for boats to come. This gave the Confederate Army time to send in 80,000 soldiers. They spread 3 miles (4.8 km) along the riverbanks.

After crossing, Burnside ordered an attack. His men broke through the Confederate lines. But Burnside did not send his troops through the hole. This was a mistake. The Confederates won a counterattack. By the end of the day, the Union Army had twice as many losses as the Confederates. Lee granted Burnside a **truce** on December 14. The armies used this time to bury their dead.

WARTIME WHISKERS General Burnside had hair on his face next to his ears. The hairs connected to his mustache. This became a new fashion for men of that time. The hairs were known as "burnsides." Today, they are known as sideburns.

Union General Ambrose Burnside

Burnside knew his troops had been beaten. That night, he called off the battle. He moved his men back across the river. This was a crushing loss for the Union. The victory boosted the Confederates' **morale**.

12,500 Number of Union Army casualties.

The Confederates lost 6,000 troops. • Burnside's troops crossed the river on December 11, 1862. • Six weeks later, President Lincoln removed Burnside from command.

A memorial in Virginia honors a soldier who cared for the wounded at Fredericksburg.

The Emancipation Proclamation *Frees Slaves*

8

At the start of the Civil War, President Lincoln had one goal. He wanted to save the Union. He was also against slavery. But he did not think he had the power to free slaves. And the nation did not agree to go to war just to end slavery.

By 1862, thousands of formerly enslaved people had escaped to the North. They were very interested in fighting for freedom. President Lincoln saw their value. There were many of them. The loss of workers weakened the Confederacy. Now, those same workers would strengthen the Union Army.

On January 1, 1863, Lincoln issued an order. It was the Emancipation Proclamation. It freed all the enslaved people in the Confederacy. It did not end slavery completely. Border states could still hold slaves. But it freed three-fourths of the enslaved people in the nation. However, the order could not be enforced during the war.

The proclamation had a huge impact on the war. If the Union won, nearly all enslaved people would be free. The order also let freed slaves join the Union forces. By the end of the war, 180,000 freed slaves had joined the Union Army. Another 10,000 joined the Union Navy.

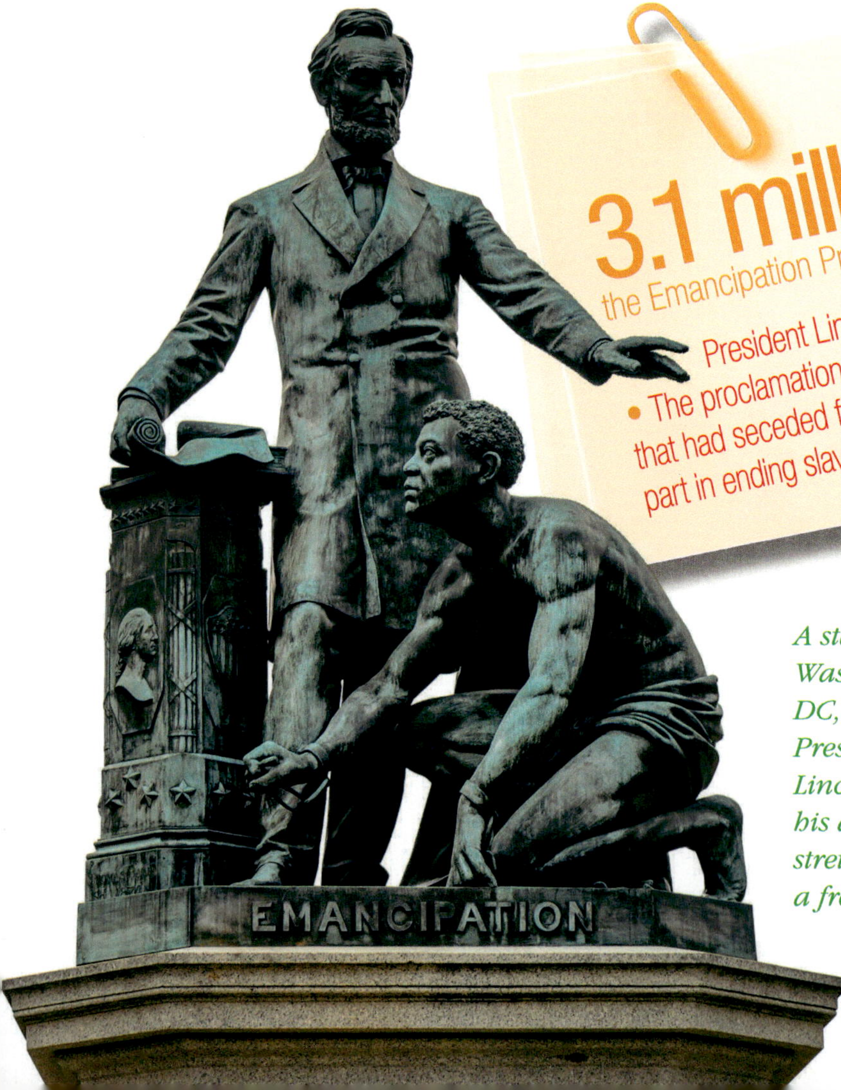

3.1 million Number of slaves who were freed by the Emancipation Proclamation.

- President Lincoln issued the order to free slaves.
- The proclamation was limited.
- It only applied to states that had seceded from the Union.
- But it played a big part in ending slavery in the United States.

A statue in Washington, DC, shows President Lincoln with his arm stretched over a freed slave.

2013
HENCEFORWARD
SHALL BE
FREE
EMANCIPATION
PROCLAMATION
ABRAHAM LINCOLN
1863
FOREVER USA

Both Sides Begin to *Draft Soldiers*

9

An unknown Union soldier is buried at Shiloh, Tennessee.

When the Civil War began, men signed up for military service. They wanted to fight. By the end of 1862, they were tired. The war had gone on for too long. But the Confederacy still needed soldiers. In April 1862, they began a **draft**. It called healthy men between ages 17 and 50 to service. Many Southerners were against this.

The Union was having problems too. It needed fresh soldiers. On March 3, 1863, Congress began a draft. This act was the first wartime draft in the country's history. All men between ages 20 and 45 had to sign up.

No one liked the draft. Some thought it was a breach of their rights. They did not want to be forced to fight. Others feared those who did not want to fight would be poor soldiers. The draft lowered morale among the troops.

Wealthy men could buy out of service. Other men paid stand-ins to fight for them. Poor men could not do either. They felt the draft was unfair. Many stand-ins left the battlefield to hire themselves out again. The Union drafted 250,000 men. Only 46,000 of them actually served.

WOMEN AND CHILDREN JOIN THE FIGHT

Many women and children were ready to join the army. Hundreds of women dressed as men to sign up. They fought secretly in both the Union and Confederate armies. Children lied about their ages in order to join the war.

Frances Clayton disguised herself as a man to join the Union army as "Jack Williams."

RECRUITS WANTED!

104TH PENNSYLVANIA

REGIMENT!

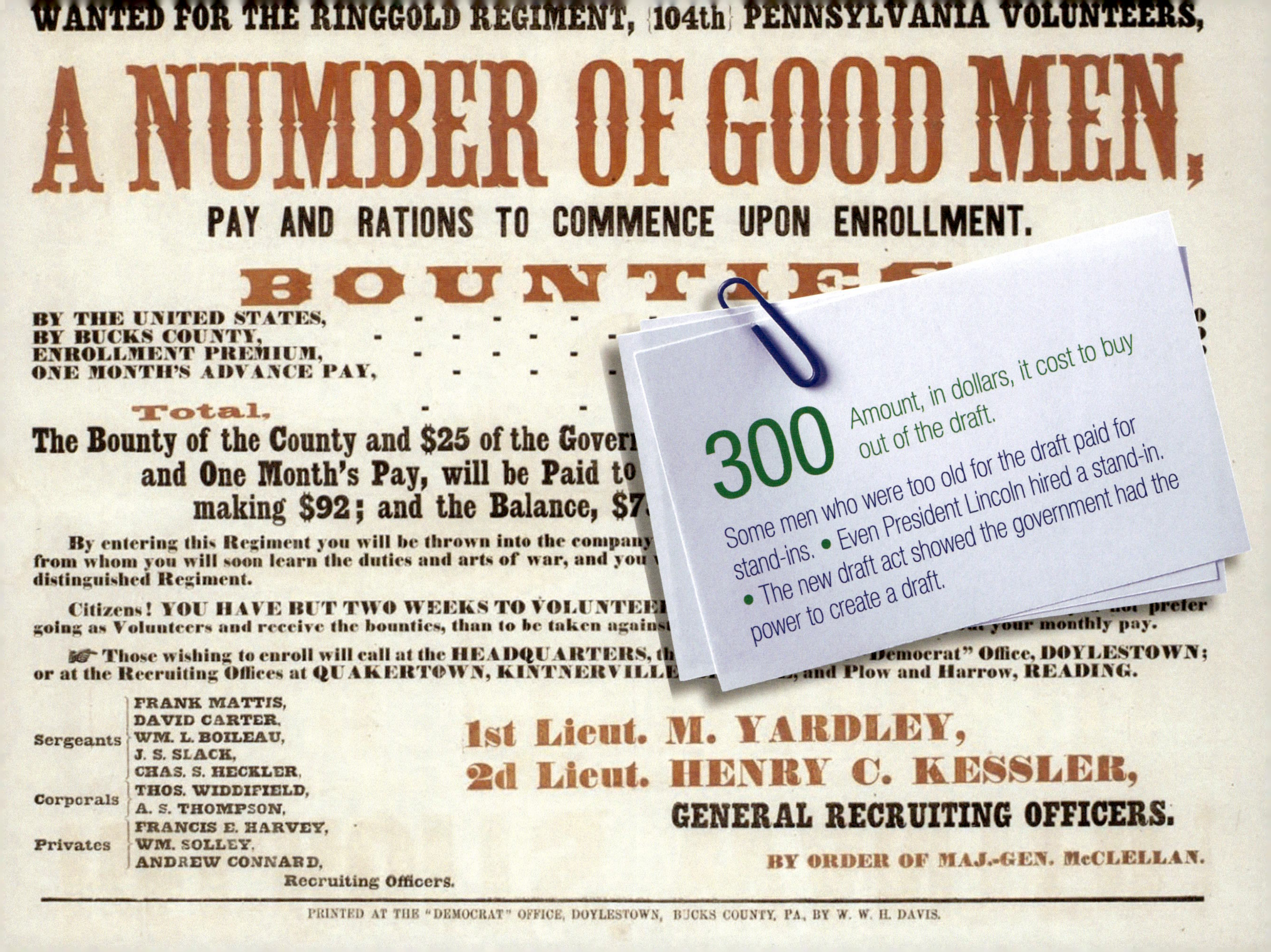

300 Amount, in dollars, it cost to buy out of the draft.

Some men who were too old for the draft paid for stand-ins. • Even President Lincoln hired a stand-in. • The new draft act showed the government had the power to create a draft.

Battle of Gettysburg Sends Confederate *Forces Home*

10 Many battles were fought in the South. Confederate General Robert E. Lee had a win at Chancellorsville, Virginia. His next move was against the North. On July 1, 1863, he marched his men into Gettysburg, Pennsylvania. They clashed with Union forces. Lee's men pushed them back. The battle went on the next day. Each side lost more than 9,000 men.

On July 3, Union forces turned the tides. They won back their position. Lee sent 15,000 soldiers across an open field. They attacked the Union Army. The Union soldiers took cover behind stone walls. Some fired from behind the walls. Others surrounded the Confederates. The Confederate division lost two-thirds of its men. The survivors fell back to their starting positions. The Union won the battle.

The Battle of Gettysburg was a turning point in the war for Union forces.

51,000 Number of casualties at Gettysburg.

The battle lasted three days. • More Americans died than in the Revolutionary War and the War of 1812 combined. • The Union had 90,000 soldiers at Gettysburg. • The Confederates had 70,000 soldiers.

On July 4, Lee waited for a Union counterattack. It never happened. That night, Lee left with his army. They marched back to Virginia.

The Battle of Gettysburg was a big loss for the South. The North had a huge advantage before the battle. It had many more resources. It had **industry** to make war weapons. It had railroads and rivers to move them. It also had 20,000 more soldiers than the South. General Lee lost more than one-third of his total army at Gettysburg. It was a turning point in the Civil War.

KILLER COLDS

More men died from diseases than wounds during the Civil War. Army camps were filthy. Diseases spread quickly. Typhoid fever killed one-fourth of the soldiers who got it. There were 1 million cases of malaria. Many men caught colds. They later died from pneumonia.

Lee Surrenders at *Appomattox*

11

By April 1865, the South was losing the war. Lee's army was at Petersburg, Virginia. They had held back the Union forces for almost 10 months. His troops were worn out. His supplies were nearly gone. Confederate President Davis had left the city. Things were looking hopeless.

Union General Ulysses S. Grant wanted to stop more bloodshed. He knew Lee's outlook was bad. On April 7, Grant reached out to Lee. He asked Lee to give up the fight. Lee stalled. He was not quite ready to do it. But he did ask for Grant's terms of surrender.

The next day, the Confederacy was beaten at Appomattox Station. On April 9, Lee accepted Grant's terms. Confederate soldiers agreed to lay down their arms. They promised to stop fighting and go home. They could keep their horses.

Confederate soldier's hat

Grant fed the hungry troops. He promised the men could travel home safely.

The formal surrender of arms took place on April 12. But the Civil War did not end that day. Other Confederate armies were still fighting. Over the next months, other leaders surrendered throughout the South. The last one gave up on November 6, 1865.

General Grant (right) discusses surrender with General Lee.

Think About It The Civil War was known by many names. Research other names for the Civil War. Choose two. Explain why you think those names were fitting.

5 Number of days from Grant's surrender until Lee's army laid down their arms.

On April 12, the formal surrender of arms took place. • On November 6, the Confederate Army made its last surrender. • The Civil War was over.

12

Reconstruction Begins

Lincoln would not live long enough to see the country be rebuilt.

On May 23, 1865, the Union celebrated the end of the Civil War. But the North and South were still divided. The torn nation needed to rebuild. This era is known as Reconstruction.

President Lincoln made a speech on April 11, 1865. He called for Black people to have the right to vote. Lincoln would not see this plan through. He was **assassinated** three days later. Vice President Andrew Johnson took over as president.

Congress passed important laws. The 13th Amendment ended slavery. In response, the Southern states created Black Codes. These laws limited the work Black people could do. The 14th Amendment passed in 1868. It gave citizenship to formerly enslaved people.

The Reconstruction Act of 1867 was the next step. It set the terms for Southern states to be admitted back into the Union. Tennessee had been readmitted the year before. But no others were brought back in until June 22, 1868. Arkansas was the first. Then five more states followed. On July 15, 1870, Georgia was the last state admitted back into the Union. At last, the nation was united again.

The last of the Union troops left the South in 1877. Reconstruction came to an end. The war was over. But the scars would remain for years to come.

John Wilkes Booth used a derringer pistol to kill President Lincoln.

Booth shot Lincoln in the back of the head at Ford's Theater in Washington, DC.

12 Key Dates

December 20, 1860
South Carolina secedes from the Union.

April 12, 1861
The Confederates fire on Fort Sumter, starting the Civil War.

April 15, 1861
Lincoln calls for 75,000 volunteers to fight in the Union Army.

February 6, 1862
The Union captures Fort Henry.

September 17, 1862
The Battle of Antietam becomes the bloodiest day in US history.

December 13, 1892
Lee wins the Battle of Fredericksburg for the Confederates.

April 12, 1861

January 1, 1863

April 15, 1861

January 1, 1863
Lincoln issues the Emancipation Proclamation.

March 3, 1863
Congress passes the first wartime draft.

July 3, 1863
The Union wins the Battle of Gettysburg.

April 12, 1865
Lee surrenders, beginning the end of the war.

November 6, 1865
The last Confederate surrender takes place.

July 15, 1870
The last Confederate state is admitted back into the Union.

November 6, 1865

July 3, 1863

Glossary

amendment
A formal or official change made to a law, constitution, or other legal document.

assassinate
To kill another person, usually for pay or from loyalty to a cause.

blockade
To seal off a place to prevent goods or people from entering or leaving.

casualty
A military person lost through death, wounds, illness, enemy capture, or who goes missing.

citizen
An inhabitant of a town or city.

compromise
A way of reaching agreement in which each group gives up something.

draft
To require a person to enlist in military service.

industry
The process of making products by using machines and factories.

insurrection
A violent uprising against a government.

morale
A maintained belief in a goal or institution, especially during difficult times.

plantation
A large area of land where crops are grown and harvested.

repeal
To officially make no longer valid.

secede
To withdraw formally from an alliance.

treason
The act of betraying someone or something.

truce
An agreement between enemies or opponents to stop fighting for a certain time.

unconstitutional
Something not allowed by the constitution of a city or government.

For More Information

Books

Moening, Kate. *The American Civil War*. Minneapolis: Bellwether Media, 2024.

Connors, Kathleen. *Q & A About the Civil War*. Buffalo, NY: Enslow Publishing, 2025.

Bearce, Stephanie. *Awesome, Disgusting, Unusual Facts about the Civil War*. Mankato, MN: Black Rabbit Books, 2024.

Gale, Ryan. *Fact and Fiction of the Civil War*. Minneapolis: Abdo Publishing, 2022.

Websites

Defining Battles of the Civil War
education.nationalgeographic.org/resource/defining-battles-civil-war/

The Battle of Gettysburg
tpt.pbslearningmedia.org/resource/gettysburg-video-9006/gettysburg-ken-burns-the-civil-war/

Crash Course US History: The Civil War
thecrashcourse.com/courses/the-civil-war-part-i-crash-course-us-history-20/

About the Author

Marne Ventura is a children's book author and a former elementary school teacher. She holds a master's degree in education with an emphasis in reading and language development from the University of California.

Index

 • Top Rank is an imprint of Black Rabbit Books. • Designed by Danny Nanos • Photographs © Alamy Stock Photo/Circa Images, 31, Niday Picture Library, 16; Dreamstime/ Georgesheldon, 22, Indy2320, 2–3, 19, James Fowler, 10, Nikkidrinkwater, 17, 20, Roger Asbury, 10, Steveheap, 37, Wayne Mckown, 39; Getty Images/Historical, 13; Library of Congress/ Anthony Berger/Brady's National Photographic Portrait Galleries, 8, Paul Philippoteaux, 34–35, 45; Shutterstock/AlessandraRC, 23, Belinda Pretorius, 48, chrisbrignell, 14, 16, 11, 44, Everett Collection, cover, 1, 27, 42–43, EWY Media, 26, 30, Gerald Villena, 36, Jolygon, 46–47, Levent Konuk, 37, Manuel Esteban, 24, Morphart Creation, 18, 21, Scott K Baker, 41, spatuletail, 29, 44, STUDIO MELANGE, 28, TonLammerts, 29, vkilikov, 40, 44, Zack Frank, 11; Wikimedia Commons/Alonzo Chappel, 2, 38, 45, Benjamin Haydon, 7, Emanuel Leutze, 25, H. L. S. L. Johnson & Co., 32–33, Henry P. Moore/New-York Historical Society, 9, Kiddo27, 5, Kurz & Allison, 15, McConnell Map Co., 4; Public Domain/Unknown, 12

Library of Congress Cataloging-in-Publication Data: Names: Ventura, Marne, author. | Title: The Civil War: 12 things to know / by Marne Ventura. | Description: Mankato, MN: Top Rank is an imprint of Black Rabbit Books, [2026] | Series: America at war | Includes bibliographical references and index. | Ages 9–13 | Grades 4–6 | Identifiers: LCCN 2024050097 (print) | LCCN 2024050098 (ebook) | ISBN 9781644668214 (library binding) | ISBN 9781644668535 (paperback) | ISBN 9781644668856 (ebook) | Subjects: LCSH: United States—History—Civil War, 1861–1865—Miscellanea—Juvenile literature. | Classification: LCC E468 .V46 2026 (print) | LCC E468 (ebook) | DDC 973.7—dc23/eng/20241129 | LC record available at https://lccn.loc.gov/2024050097